Wise Ben

by Andrew Huffman
illustrated by Jane Newman

Harcourt

Orlando   Boston   Dallas   Chicago   San Diego

Visit *The Learning Site!*

www.harcourtschool.com

Benjamin Franklin's life is truly a rags-to-riches story. Ben Franklin was born poor and died rich, fulfilling what might be called the American dream. His wealth was the result of his own effort and hard work. Throughout his life, Ben never stopped working. In fact, he seems to have followed the advice of one of his own sayings: "The used key is always bright."

Born in Boston in 1706, he was the fifteenth of seventeen children. By the time he was born, some of his older brothers and sisters were already grown and out of the house. Still, he remembered a time when his parents had thirteen children around the dinner table.

That's a lot of children to feed! It's not surprising that Ben's father couldn't afford to send him to school. All together, Ben had only two years of formal schooling, starting at the age of eight. The rest of his education came from his own reading.

His formal education was suspended when he was ten. He was taken out of school to help in his father's business. He worked long hours, often twelve to fourteen hours a day, making soap and candles. Ben would not have minded the long hours if he had enjoyed the work. What he really wanted was to become a sailor.

Ben's father did not want him to be a sailor. One of Ben's older brothers had already died at sea, and his father did not want to lose another son. So, at the age of twelve, Ben became an apprentice to his brother, James. Ben would learn to be a printer.

A few years later, when Ben was about fifteen, James began his own newspaper. Ben helped to print and sell the paper.

In 1722, Ben began writing a series of fourteen articles in the form of letters to his brother's paper. He thought that his brother would reject the articles if he knew who the author was. So he used a different name. He slipped the letters under the door of the printing shop at night, and his brother published them.

These letters, which were very humorous, were very popular with the readers. They made fun of Boston society, politics, and religion. Everyone was surprised to find out that the widow Silence Dogood, the "author" of the letters, was really Ben Franklin himself! He was a published writer at the age of sixteen.

Ben grew tired of working for his brother, so he left Boston in 1723. He traveled by boat to Philadelphia to seek his own fortune. When he got there, he was tired and hungry after the long trip. The first thing he did was find a bakery and order three pennies' worth of bread.

Philadelphia

Prices were low in Philadelphia, and he got more bread than he had expected. He walked out of the bakery with "three great puffy rolls," as he said in his *Autobiography*. Because his pockets were stuffed with socks and shirts (he didn't have a suitcase), he had no place to put the rolls.

He carried one under each arm as he ate the third. As he walked from the Market Street wharf, he aroused the interest of many people. One of them was Deborah Read, who would later become his wife.

Ben continued walking and eating his roll until he found himself back at the wharf. By then, he had eaten enough. He gave away the other two rolls to a woman and her child who had been on the boat with him.

Within a few days, Ben got a job with a printer in Philadelphia. A few years later, he opened his own print shop. He printed *The Pennsylvania Gazette*, a very successful newspaper.

At about this time, Ben decided that he wanted to improve himself. He said that he "wished to live without committing any fault any time." So he wrote a list of thirteen virtues that he wanted to practice in his life.

Here are the first six virtues on that list, as well as his directions to himself:

1. TEMPERANCE. Eat not to dullness; drink not to elevation.
2. SILENCE. Speak not but what may benefit others or yourself; avoid trifling conversation.
3. ORDER. Let all your things have their places; let each part of your business have its time.
4. RESOLUTION. Resolve to perform what you ought; perform without fail what you resolve.
5. FRUGALITY. Make no expense but to do good to others or yourself; i.e., waste nothing.
6. INDUSTRY. Lose no time; be always employed in something useful; cut off all unnecessary actions.

Other virtues on his list urged him to be sincere, fair, moderate, clean, and peaceful. The last virtue on his list was humility. He later said that he was not very successful with this virtue. All the honors that he received in his life perhaps made it hard for him to be humble.

In 1733, Ben Franklin published the first edition of an almanac under the name of Richard Saunders. He called it *Poor Richard's Almanack*. Except for the Bible, the *Almanack* became the best-selling book in the colonies. Publication of this almanac was not suspended until twenty-five years later.

Each edition of *Poor Richard's Almanack* was a calendar full of ads, weather forecasts, recipes, jokes, and sayings. Those sayings are still popular today. Here are some of the most famous of them:

- A rolling stone gathers no moss.
- Honesty is the best policy.
- A penny saved is a penny earned.
- Early to bed and early to rise makes a man healthy, wealthy, and wise.
- God helps them that help themselves.
- Lost time is never found again.
- There are no gains without pains.
- He that goes a-borrowing goes a-sorrowing.
- Never leave that till tomorrow which you can do today.

Ben Franklin did not believe in wasting money on foolish things. He was frugal and thrifty. He saved his money and made wise investments. By the time he was forty-two, he had generated enough of a fortune to retire.

Retirement for Ben Franklin did not mean resting. Retirement gave him a chance to explore things that really interested him. He became involved in public service, science, and politics.

Following his own rule to "be always employed in something useful," he looked around Philadelphia. He was looking for what needed to be done to make the city a better place.

He had noticed that much of the heat from a fireplace was lost up the chimney. He invented a contraption that is still in use today. It was an iron box that fit into the opening of the fireplace. As the iron sides of the box get hot from the fire, they spread the heat around the room.

Franklin called it the Pennsylvania Fire Place, but everyone else soon called the contraption the Franklin Stove. If he had taken out a patent on it, he could have made a lot of money. A patent protects the inventor's

right to be the only one to make and sell the product. Franklin did not want a patent. Instead, he said he was "glad of an opportunity to serve others."

Ben went on to serve his country by acting as a diplomat in England during colonial times. The colonists wanted England to repeal certain unfair taxes. Ben was success-ful in getting England to repeal some of these taxes, but then England imposed others. Although he tried his best to prevent tension over the taxes from turning into a war, he could not. He wrote to a friend, "There never was a good war or a bad peace."

Paris

Years later, when the Revolutionary War was ending, Ben Franklin was asked to help write the peace treaty. Because it was written in Paris, where Ben was then living, it was called the Treaty of Paris.

Ben Franklin enjoyed many honors during his lifetime. But what he enjoyed most was working to understand and to improve the world around him.